Original title:
The Green Room Chronicles

Copyright © 2025 Creative Arts Management OÜ
All rights reserved.

Author: Clara Whitfield
ISBN HARDBACK: 978-1-80581-872-4
ISBN PAPERBACK: 978-1-80581-399-6
ISBN EBOOK: 978-1-80581-872-4

Unraveled Threads of Greenery

In a garden where vines pretzel and twist,
A gopher plays poker, you get the gist.
The daisies are gossiping, oh what a scene,
As tomatoes debate who is juicier, keen.

A hedgehog in sunglasses sips lemonade,
While worms form a band and dance in the shade.
The daisies declare they're the queens of the lot,
But the dandelions laugh, 'We all know you're not!'

The Garden Intermission

Butterflies flutter with sass in the air,
While bunnies are searching for edible flair.
The marigolds chuckle at garden gnomes,
Who just stood in silence as they roam like phone homes.

A frog wearing slippers jumps from a high rock,
While snails take their time; it's always o'clock.
In this patch of green, every critter's a star,
Even the worms dream of life in a jar!

Echoing Through the Leaves

The wind tells a tale to the old weeping tree,
Of squirrels who argue, 'This nut belongs to me!'
A flower pot cracked, and it started to sing,
As everything laughed at the joy it would bring.

The wind chimes are clinking, and voices abound,
While ladybugs march like a troupe in the round.
In this green hideaway, there's fun all around,
Even the quietest grass makes a sound!

Dreaming in a Glistening Grove

In a grove where the crickets compose the night song,
A raccoon in pajamas is singing along.
Leaves whisper secrets in a playful tease,
As fireflies twinkle like stars in the breeze.

The cupcakes are baking with fairy dust sprinkles,
While mushrooms conspire, sharing their twinkles.
Every corner holds laughter, a whimsical show,
In this sweet little hideout where mischief will grow!

Tapestry of Botanical Voices

In the corner sits a fern,
With secrets no one knows,
It giggles at the daisies,
As their beauty surely grows.

A cactus tells a joke,
Spikes and wit combined,
The orchids roll their eyes,
While laughing, they unwind.

The ivy climbs the walls,
Whispering tales of cheer,
It chats with all the roses,
Their thorns a light veneer.

In this garden of mirth,
No serious talk allowed,
The plants hold court with laughter,
And they're always quite proud.

Shadows of Forgotten Performances

Underneath the stage light,
The dust bunnies take a bow,
Their ballet moves are timid,
But they still take a vow.

A forgotten script in hand,
The moths do their best show,
With fluttering pirouettes,
They steal the evening glow.

In corners where it's dark,
The soda cans hold sway,
They clink as if to cheer,
For actors lost today.

The spotlight's gone to sleep,
But the laughter echoes still,
In shadows where we wait,
For the next big thrill.

Lush Labyrinths of Memory

In a maze of tangled thoughts,
A squirrel's got a plan,
He brings the nuts of laughter,
To share with every fan.

A hedgehog with a mic,
Sings off-key to the tune,
His audience of flowers,
Are swaying with the moon.

Beneath the leafy boughs,
Old jokes resound anew,
The pathways twist and turn,
In pastel shades and hue.

With every corner turned,
A giggle grows more strong,
In labyrinths of laughter,
We dance the whole night long.

Serenade for a Silent Audience

The walls are thin with whispers,
Of silence held so tight,
Each note a nervous chuckle,
That dances in the night.

A turtle sings ballads,
With a shell of rhymes and glee,
His audience, untouched grass,
Grows a little tipsy tree.

With shadows as conductors,
They sway without a sound,
In the quiet of the evening,
A symphony is found.

So here's to all the giggles,
That rise in whispered tones,
For every silent audience,
Deserves a laugh of their own.

Syllables of the Sun-Dappled Hideaway

In a nook of bright delight,
Laughter dances, oh, what a sight!
Chairs that wobble, tables sing,
Here's to joy that awkwardly swings.

Sun-kissed beams on walls so green,
Funny whispers, what a scene!
A cat that struts with regal flair,
Chasing shadows without a care.

Mismatched socks and silly hats,
Coffee spills and friendly chats.
In this space, the quirks align,
Every moment, a punchline divine.

So let us toast with mugs held high,
To comic tales that never die!
In the sun-dappled hideaway bright,
Every giggle feels just right.

Parables of the Climbing Ivy

Up the walls, the ivy climbs,
With curious twists and silly rhymes.
It knows secrets of the breeze,
Whispering jokes through rustling leaves.

A squirrel stumbles, then it grins,
Finding acorns where fun begins.
Jumping high, a daring feat,
The world laughs back—oh, what a treat!

Adventures in a leafy maze,
As mischief weaves through sunny rays.
Tangled tales of joy goodbye,
In the heart, the ivy's high.

So gather 'round this bumpy ride,
With ivy laughter as our guide.
In every twist and wooden beam,
We find the spark of a shared dream.

Whispers in the Painted Shadows

In the corners, shadows play,
Whispers giggle, come out and sway!
Each hue dances, a lively jest,
In this space, we're all guests.

A knock-knock joke from a splashed wall,
Painted stories that rise and fall.
Under bright lights, shadows tease,
Funny tales float on the breeze.

With every brushstroke, laughter glows,
Crayon critters, oh how they pose!
A canvas of chuckles hangs so wide,
As silly fables take us for a ride.

So come and laugh in this vivid light,
Where whispers tickle us every night.
In painted shadows, we all belong,
Celebrating joy in our silly song.

Echoes of a Verdant Stage

On this stage of leafy greens,
Actors fumble, break routines.
A parrot squawks the wrong cue,
Laughter rolls like morning dew.

With every scene, a pratfall grand,
A garden gnome takes a stand.
Costumes made of twigs and leaves,
Invisible tricks up their sleeves.

The spotlight shines on a toad's dance,
As flowers sway, they take their chance.
Echoes of giggles fill the air,
In this verdant space, we all share.

Curtains rustle, bows are made,
From every blunder, memories laid.
In this theater of green delight,
We find the fun, both day and night.

Dialogue Among the Dappled Shadows

Under branches, sunlight plays,
Squirrels gossip, oh what a craze!
Whispers float, secrets shared,
With acorns tossed, not a soul spared.

Mice wearing hats, a curious sight,
Dancing in circles, oh what delight!
Tails intertwined, a waltz in the grass,
Laughter erupts, as they trip and amass.

A snail with glasses reads us a tale,
About a frog who tried to sail.
Swapping jokes, the trees sway,
Echoing chuckles that brighten the day.

Birds chirp punchlines, all in good jest,
Nature's stand-up, they know how to fest!
Amidst the laughter in dappled light,
The shadows grin, all feeling just right.

The Echoing Arbor

In the grove, a party swells,
Breezes carry the echoes of yells.
Tag team friendships, mossy and spry,
Each branch a witness, watching them fly.

Chattering leaves, gossip so fine,
A squirrel claims the best acorn's mine!
"Ode to the Bumpy", the beetles sing,
While ants parade with a potted spring.

Foxes in tuxes, what a fine scene,
Twirling their tails, oh how they preen!
Laughter like raindrops on thirsty ground,
In this echo chamber, joy shall abound.

As day fades away into twilight mist,
The shadows dance, how could they resist?
Nature joins in the humor parade,
In this lively patch, none are afraid.

When Leaves Speak

When leaves talk, they crack a grin,
Rustling tales of where they've been.
A branch with humor, stories abound,
Of sudden gusts that spun them around.

A caterpillar jokes in a slow, wise tone,
"By tomorrow, I'll be climbing alone!"
The younger buds laugh, fueled by dreams,
In this shady space, nothing's as it seems.

A chattering brook joins in the fun,
Flowing with laughter, a race just begun.
With every ripple, a giggle escapes,
As dragonflies leap in colorful shapes.

Under the moon, as shadows befriend,
The leaves whisper softly, "This laughter won't end!"
With a chuckle or two, the night takes a bow,
Inviting all creatures to join in right now.

Fables of the Lush Haven

In a land where laughter blooms,
Every corner hums with funny tunes.
The sunbeams tickle each blooming sprout,
As bees crack jokes—no doubt about!

A wise old tortoise tells tales of old,
Of misfit friends, and their antics bold.
"Once I raced a hare, too quick, too spry,
But tripped on my shell—oh me, oh my!"

Butterflies flutter, with giggles so light,
Swapping stories, dancing in flight.
Mushrooms cheer and mushrooms groan,
As crickets play tunes for the roots they've sown.

Under the canopy, mirth finds its way,
In this lush haven, come join the play.
With laughter entwined in the fabric of green,
Each fable here is a humor-filled scene.

Secrets of the Hidden Grove

In the grove where whispers play,
Squirrels plot their grand ballet.
Mice wear hats, so dapper too,
They toast with acorns, just a few.

Beneath the branches, shadows prance,
Frogs in tuxedos start to dance.
A raccoon juggles shiny things,
While owls gossip, flap their wings.

Nutty tales from creatures small,
Each secret shared, they have a ball.
Tales of owls, moonlit schemes,
And how to catch the sweetest dreams.

In the hidden grove of cheer,
Every laugh rings loud and clear.
The merry band is quite a sight,
In leafy realms of pure delight.

Melodies in the Moss

Beneath the boughs where shadows hum,
Fungi sing, and drummers strum.
A whispered tune, soft and sweet,
Beetles tap their tiny feet.

The melodies from mossy hearts,
Ring out like the best of arts.
Crickets croon, while spiders weave,
A harmony that won't deceive.

Fireflies clutch their glowing notes,
As snails belt out their funny quotes.
In this concert, all are stars,
No need for fancy guitars.

So join the fun beneath the leaves,
Where every creature truly believes.
A symphony that's hard to miss,
In the moss, a world of bliss.

Tales from the Emerald Corridor

In corridors of vibrant green,
Wombats roll, a funny scene.
Old hedgehogs act like stand-up news,
While butterflies don fancy shoes.

Each turn reveals a comic twist,
A tale of a snail who can't be kissed.
Raccoons with dreams of grand ballet,
Prancing 'round without delay.

Each shade of green holds joyful sighs,
As critters plot their clever lies.
An anteater, late for tea,
Trips on a leaf, oh what a spree!

Emerald tales, a blend of glee,
Join in the laughter, feel the spree.
In this corridor of delight,
Each day's an unexpected flight.

Notes from a Forgotten Play

On stage of leaves where dreams reside,
The rabbits take their turns with pride.
A sly old fox, a script in paw,
Recites the lines, but forgets the law.

The mushrooms cheer, the crickets chime,
Was that a jest or just a rhyme?
Lost lines scattered in the breeze,
As hedgehogs shout, "Please, oh please!"

In this play where few take note,
A butterfly flit, a goat that wrote.
With every act, they lead with flair,
In this forgotten theater air.

So grab a seat, the fun won't stop,
As laughing leaves take center top.
In this tale, both wild and free,
Each misstep turns to comedy.

A Waiting Room of Leaves

In a room of verdant hue,
The ferns all wear a curious view.
A gossiping tree shares a tale,
While caterpillars cruise like a sail.

The chairs are made of twisted vines,
With cushions stuffed with leafy signs.
A snail arrives dressed like a queen,
Sipping dew from a cups of green.

The clocks tick in a slothful maze,
With every minute filled with praise.
While ants play poker, small and spry,
Their laughter echoes, oh so sly.

As sunlight dances, shadows sway,
The room feels lively, come what may.
With nature's jokes in every crevice,
The waiting game becomes a circus.

Twilight's Gentle Reverie

As twilight whispers to the trees,
The crickets hum tune-like, with ease.
A firefly holds a little ball,
While grasshoppers dance, oh what a call!

The moon peeks in, a silver grin,
As frogs croak out their nightly din.
A raccoon juggles acorn treats,
While laughter swirls on twinkling beats.

Clouds play tag with the starlit spark,
Once or twice, they miss the mark.
The breeze carries secrets now,
While night-time creatures take a bow.

In this soft glow, joy takes flight,
With giggles echoing through the night.
The world awaits the dawn anew,
As dreams arise in shades of blue.

The Hidden Heartbeat

In the shade of a willow's arm,
A secret hum, a gentle charm.
Bees conduct their buzzing choir,
While ants hold meetings by the fire.

A badger's wit is sharp and keen,
He cracks a joke, the loudest scene.
While rabbits chuckle, rolling round,
In this heartbeat, joy is found.

Underneath the tangled brush,
Laughter grows in every hush.
A squirrel winks with mischief grand,
As laughter covers all the land.

With every rustle, hearts align,
Nature's humor is quite divine.
In silent moments, whimsy plays,
As the hidden heartbeat sways.

Enigma of the Emerald Stage

On a stage where flowers bloom,
The petals gossip, avoiding gloom.
A snail performs a slow ballet,
And mushrooms cheer in bright display.

The ivy vines wrap tight in cheers,
As laughter drowns out all the fears.
A beetle takes up the mic to sing,
While frogs throw leaves, it's a wild fling.

The stars twinkle, clapping in joy,
As crickets strut, a rhythmic ploy.
Each creature writes a tale of jest,
In emerald hues, they find their rest.

So gather round to share the laugh,
In this world of the thin green path.
With every moment, a silly game,
This enigma fuels the nature's flame.

A Scene Without an Actor

The curtains hang, a silent throng,
A chair on stage, where it feels wrong.
Props gather dust, on a lonely shelf,
The spotlight waits for a different self.

An empty role, a laugh or two,
The ghost of comedy, winks at you.
A sock onstage, it steals the show,
With visions grand where no one can go.

A witty mishap, a pratfall missed,
The popcorn's quiet, a twisted twist.
With shadows dancing, where laughter's bare,
The show must go on—it's just not there!

A setup ready with no one to play,
The audience stares, in disarray.
A scene without an actor's wit,
Turns life's own chaos into a skit.

Echoes of an Emerald Past

In the rafters, whispers carry light,
Ghostly echoes of a leafy night.
A vine entwined with tales to tell,
Of mishaps, tumbles, and ups as well.

Actors pranced in verdant dreams,
But the lettuce laughed at their schemes.
Cabbages rolled in comedic glee,
While broccoli chuckled, 'Ah, 'twas me!'

A throwback to costumes made of grass,
The punchlines sprouted and grew with sass.
As clovers clapped, and daisies told,
Stories of mishaps, both brave and bold.

So gather 'round and lend an ear,
To roots of laughter that once were near.
In emerald echoes, the fun won't fade,
As laughter grows where sarcasm's played.

The Leafy Requiem

Beneath the boughs, a somber game,
An acorn's plight, a leaf's one claim.
They gather round, in silence deep,
To mourn the greens that take a leap.

A lettuce helmet, worn askew,
Saluted near the avocado stew.
Zen garden jokes, all in a row,
As parsnips whisper, 'What do you know?'

A carrot sings in monotone,
'Oh, leafy friends, we're not alone!'
With each old tale, the humor shines,
In this strange requiem, laughter combines.

So raise a glass of berry brew,
To leafy legends that once felt blue.
With every wink, and every quip,
The requiem dances, a lively trip.

Stories on a Green Palette

In a garden nook where stories bloom,
The veggies jest, dispelling gloom.
A squash with wit, and a potato sly,
As kohlrabi quips, 'Just watch me fly!'

Underneath the kale, a secret plot,
Tomatoes burst with laughter hot.
'Why did the beet refuse to race?'
'Because it knew it wouldn't keep pace!'

Peas in a pod sharing a laugh,
Of misfit seeds in a leafy craft.
Olive branches wave at tales precise,
As sprouting dreams roll the dice.

So take a seat, grab a green drink,
Dive into tales that make you think.
On this palette of laughter, take your part,
For each vibrant story is pure heart.

The Quiet Performance

In the corner, a squirrel's on stage,
Scratching his head like a wise old sage.
The crowd of ants in a fervent hush,
Waiting for chaos, everything's a rush.

A snail rolls in with a dramatic flair,
His shell filled with snacks, quite the rare fare.
The audience gasps, but then they all cheer,
For every slow act brings laughter, oh dear!

With a wink and a shimmy, the beetles all dance,
Strutting their stuff, not leaving to chance.
The grass starts to rustle, a tickling breeze,
This show has no end, just joy and a tease.

As curtains of leaves start to rustle and sway,
The finale's approaching, hip hip hooray!
When the applause echoes through the dark night,
The quiet performance ends with delight.

Dancers in the Dew

Morning light spills like a golden beam,
On petals that twinkle, a beautiful dream.
With droplets like diamonds, each blade's a stage,
Tiny dancers arrive, ready to engage.

A ladybug waltzes, her spots all aglow,
While crickets create sounds that ebb and flow.
The thrill of the dew, a shimmering sight,
Their moves are so smooth, it's pure delight.

The caterpillar quivers, unsure of the groove,
His two-step is awkward, but still he will move.
Bees buzz in rhythm, a busy ballet,
Together they twirl, come join the display!

As the sun climbs higher, the curtain descends,
The dancers retire, but the laughter extends.
They bow to the blossoms, so sweet and so true,
In the morning's soft light, with joy they bid adieu.

Stagecraft of the Natural World

With branches as beams and vines as the ropes,
The forest transforms, crafting whimsical hopes.
Here, nature's the theater, with whispers and rustles,
Where even the smallest creature flexes its muscles.

The moon is the spotlight, the stars are the team,
Enhancing the scenes with a silvery gleam.
A frog leaps for laughter, a crow makes a jest,
In this lively spectacle, they all play their best.

The wind writes the script, with a flutter and flair,
While shadows dance wildly, without a care.
A punchline arrives with a sudden loud croak,
The audience chuckles, it's nature's own joke!

As the curtain of night draws slowly away,
The actors fade gently, at the end of the play.
With a final bow, they take their own flight,
In this grand production, humor takes flight.

The Canopy's Soliloquy

Up in the branches, where leaves twist and twine,
A wise old owl proclaims, 'It's my time to shine!'
In a hush of excitement, the squirrels all stare,
As he ponders his lines with a comical flair.

'What's black and white and flies like a kite?
A panda on vacation, now isn't that right?'
The crowd erupts in laughter, all critters agree,
Nature's own humor, as clear as can be.

A chattering parrot throws jokes from the boughs,
While raccoons clap paws, oh, they take their bows.
With puns and with giggles, the canopy sings,
Their laughter as light as the joy that it brings.

As dusk settles softly, the stars start to pry,
The wise owl concludes with a wink and a sigh.
In the magic of night, the tales of the trees,
Resound with the laughter carried on the breeze.

Portraits of the Enchanted Glade

In the glade where fairies play,
A squirrel wears a hat, they say.
He strikes a pose by the old oak tree,
While laughing gnomes shout, "Look at me!"

A hedgehog spins like it's ballet,
And frogs in suits dance night away.
With flowers singing silly tunes,
The moonlight sparkles, bright as balloons.

Each portrait tells a tale so sweet,
Of mischief and fun, can't take a seat.
The critters giggle, day turns night,
In this enchanted place of pure delight.

So come and see this painted crowd,
Where every laugh is joyfully loud.
An art exhibit made of cheer,
In every corner—giggles near!

Reveries Under the Twinkling Vines

Under the twinkling vines so bright,
A lazy cat naps, a comical sight.
A bird with glasses reads a book,
While snails shoot past—take a look!

The mushrooms chuckle, jokes abound,
As giggling fairies dance around.
With candy clouds and lemonade,
These silly dreams are lightly laid.

A rabbit juggles carrots tall,
While sleepy butterflies begin to crawl.
This lovely chaos, pure and wild,
Even makes the cacti smile, the child!

In reveries of laughter, dreams convene,
Adventures found where hearts are keen.
So linger here, under the sun,
For every moment's just pure fun!

The Chamber of Treasures Green

In the chamber filled with shiny things,
A frog stands guard, while a sparrow sings.
With treasures piled both high and wide,
A fox in a monocle takes a ride.

A goldfish wears a tiny crown,
As giggly whispers swirl around.
With silver spoons that dance in glee,
A parrot squawks, "Take a look at me!"

Each knickknack holds a wacky tale,
Of misadventures on a grand scale.
The fairy lights buzz with electricity,
As playful chaos becomes decree.

So in this room of laughter's haul,
All creatures gather, big and small.
With every trinket a story to glean,
This is the world that stays evergreen!

Chasing Shadows in Verdant Corners

In verdant corners, shadows play,
A hedgehog rides a snail today.
With giggles high and laughter clear,
They chase the wiggly worms near here.

A mischievous breeze carries whispers light,
As mice in sneakers prepare for flight.
With minty pie cooling on the grass,
A raccoon spies, hoping to pass.

The shadows twist and turn with glee,
While owls hoot jokes in harmony.
A game of tag in this lush, green vale,
With every tumble, they leave a trail.

So join the chase, don't be shy,
In these verdant corners, let laughter fly.
With whimsy woven through the trees,
Chasing shadows brings such sweet ease!

The Grove's Lament

In the grove where whispers thrive,
Mossy secrets come alive.
Squirrels armed with acorn flair,
Throwing shade without a care.

The trees gossip, bending low,
While flowers put on quite a show.
A bold bee dons a tiny crown,
Watch it buzz around the town.

A frog croaks jokes of grand design,
As crickets tune their silly line.
With snickers hidden in the grass,
The afternoon hours seem to pass.

And yet, beneath this leafy dome,
They plot a scheme, a nature's tome.
For every laugh, a plot twists wide,
In the grove where secrets hide.

Secrets Beneath the Stage Lights

Amidst the glow where shadows play,
The plants hold secrets in bouquet.
A cactus struts with prickly pride,
While daisies giggle, feet denied.

In corners dark, the ferns conspire,
Whispering tales of height and fire.
An oak's bark boasts of heights so near,
While violets snicker, 'What's to fear?'

The spotlight shines on blooms so bright,
Yet petals plot beneath the light.
'We're comets!' they declare in mirth,
'Who needs the sky for all we're worth?'

With every laugh, a petal falls,
As actors hide behind their walls.
For backstage bloomers love the fray,
In their own leafy cabaret.

Botanicals in the Wings

In the wings, what mischief brews,
With plants that plot, and root for duels.
A sunflower juggles with great flair,
While ivy laughs, 'There's room to spare!'

Greenery dressed in costume grand,
Whirling tunes with a leafy band.
Petunias tease the roses red,
'Last place? You're better off, we said!'

They swap their pots and hats at play,
While dandelions prank, 'It's our day!'
With giggles sprouting through the seams,
In hindsight, all had wild dreams.

For each intention that they sow,
Brings laughter's bloom, a vibrant show.
Between the leaves, the fun ignites,
As botany bursts on lazy nights.

Silences Spun in Verdancy

Amidst the quiet, greens conspire,
In whispers soft that spark a fire.
A geranium hums an off-key tune,
As leafy laughter fills the room.

With every breath, the ferns will sigh,
As moths repeat the gossip nigh.
A timid vine, it twirls with glee,
Daring all to join the spree!

Their secrets float like pollen dreams,
In packets small of laughter's beams.
The silent grace of every leaf,
In growing tales, they'll catch belief.

So gather close, dear greens unite,
In verdancy's spun delight.
For even silence has its jest,
In nature's realm, we're all a guest.

Whispers of the Verdant Veil

In a garden where laughter grows,
A gnome wears socks with silly bows.
The flowers gossip, bloom and sway,
Sharing secrets in a playful way.

A rabbit jumps, in shoes too tight,
Runs from a squirrel, ready to bite.
The sun winks down, causing a fuss,
As bees start buzzing, making a rush.

The vines entwine in a dance so fine,
While vines brag of their climbing line.
A toad in a hat croaks with flair,
Jokes with the frogs about world affairs.

Through laughter and fun, the day drifts by,
Each leaf a witness to their sly lie.
In this lush realm where mischief reigns,
The joy of nature sails like trains.

Shadows in the Emerald Lair

In a thicket, shadows play so neat,
While squirrels throw nuts, thinking it's sweet.
One chases another up a tree,
Laughing at their antics, wild and free.

A raccoon with a mischievous grin,
Snoops through the stash, thinking he'll win.
He's caught by the owl, wise and shrewd,
With a wink and a hoot, he sets the mood.

The wind whispers tales of pranks at night,
As fireflies flash their little lights.
A fox plays tricks on a bragging hare,
Says, "Try to catch me, if you dare!"

And when the sun dips low in the west,
The forest laughs, it knows what's best.
In this emerald lair, joy takes the stage,
In a world where silliness is all the rage.

Secrets Behind the Curtain of Leaves

Behind the leaves, where whispers dwell,
A turtle spins tales, oh can he tell!
Of olden days and bandit raids,
When rabbits and foxes made their parades.

A chipmunk frets, with hastily stored nuts,
"Did I hoard enough?" he ponder and struts.
The others all laugh, they know he'll see,
Hoard more than enough, that's their decree.

The sunbeams weave like dancers bright,
As bugle flowers bloom in pure delight.
A raccoon and a deer share a laugh,
In games of tag on joy's green path.

Secrets fly like leaves in a storm,
In a world where mischief is the norm.
The curtain of leaves flutters with glee,
In this realm of shenanigans, wild and free.

The Alchemist's Grove

In a grove where potions bubble and brew,
A madcap wizard wears mismatched shoes.
His cauldron spills over with giggles and cheer,
While cats in top hats pirouette near.

A bat flits by with a twinkle in eye,
Spelling spells that make daisies fly.
The mushrooms dance underfoot so spry,
While a hedgehog juggles, oh my, oh my!

"To turn rocks to snacks!" he shouts with glee,
"Isn't that a splendid recipe?"
He tosses a sprout, watches it giggle,
And the herbs in the back start to wiggle.

At night, the stars chuckle down low,
As the creatures engage in a wild show.
In this alchemist's realm, laughter is key,
Where magic is simple and joy runs free.

The Stage of Feeling

On stage, my sock puppet sings loud,
With a voice like a crow, it draws a crowd.
But when its zipper gets stuck on the floor,
The giggles and laughs start to roar.

In a pie-eating contest, I'm quite the champ,
With whipped cream slathered on my lamp.
Too much s'mores and then I just snore,
Who knew comedy's rooted in sugar galore?

A frog in a tutu does the cha-cha,
While the audience chuckles, "Oh, what a drama!"
The curtains all flap as backstage gets wild,
What's next, a seal doing tricks? Oh, it's styled!

So slide back the curtains, let the laughter fly,
The stage is a place where silliness lies.
With quirks and odd tales that make us feel free,
Join in the fun, grab a snack, and just be!

Palette of the Untold

Colors collide on a canvas so bright,
A green giraffe paints at the speed of light.
It mixes up blues with a splash of pink,
And suddenly, everyone starts to think.

A quokka walks in, holding a brush,
Splatters of ketchup, oh, there's quite the rush.
"Is ketchup a color?" it asks with a grin,
"On this palette, it's the best shade to be in!"

An octopus enters, its limbs in a twist,
Making fine art look like a fishy mist.
It juggles some paint and a ball made of cheese,
While the audience shouts for an encore, "Oh please!"

So paint all your dreams in colors so wild,
Let's blend every whim, unleash every child.
With laughter and chaos that adds to the thrill,
In this wild masterpiece, may your heart feel fulfilled!

Dialogues in Green

A cactus and fern had a chat by the stream,
Oh, the stories they told were a wild, wacky dream.
"I can hold my own water," said the prickly old chap,
"While you're just a pretty plant sitting on a map."

The daisies joined in with a petal-filled boast,
"We've got the best view, we're the garden's toast!"
But the weeds in the background, not wanting to play,
Clomped down the path, shouting, "Hey, don't dismay!"

In this garden debate, the laughter flows free,
While butterflies giggle at the new greenery.
A dandelion whispers, "Let's not fight, let's bloom,"
For the punchline's the joy that fills every room!

So here's to the dialogues that spring from the roots,
Each plant has a tale, a laugh, and some hoots.
Unite in this green, let your smiles intertwine,
In the garden of laughter, we're all doing fine!

The Prelude to Nature's Play

As dawn peeks in, the forest wears a crown,
A squirrel's got nuts and is running around.
It's a race with the breeze, they're quite the pair,
Jumping over logs, scattering everywhere!

A butterfly flutters by, wearing a hat,
Says, "Don't you dare squash me, I'm not just a brat!"
It twirls in the air, with flair and finesse,
"Take photos, not petals, I'm stylish, I guess!"

The raccoons are lurking, rehearsing a scene,
Planning a play with props made of green.
"Should we steal some snacks?" one whispers with glee,
"Only if we act like they won't notice me!"

So gather 'round nature for a comedic show,
Where the punchlines are wild and the laughter will glow.
In this prelude of nature, every critter plays cool,
In the theater of trees, it's the best-silly school!

The Hidden Scene

Behind the curtain, whispers giggle,
A cat in a hat starts to wiggle.
The stage is a mess, props all askew,
Audience waits for something quite new.

A chicken with shades struts by with flair,
The spotlight's on him, but he doesn't care.
A tap dance begins with flopping feet,
And a rubber chicken that can't find its beat.

The jester's phone rings, causing a scare,
It's a pizza delivery, folks, beware!
Confetti falls as they start to dance,
Each slip and trip—at least they took a chance.

The audience laughs, some wipe a tear,
As props get tangled, they cheer from their seat.
In this hidden scene, all is absurd,
And laughter erupts, it's simply preferred.

Fables Among the Ferns

In the ferns, squirrels chat, with so much to say,
A tale of a turtle who lost his way.
He spent a week napping under the sun,
Woke up quite grumpy, missed all the fun.

A rabbit with glasses, quite scholarly now,
Said, 'That's what you get, just look at the cow!'
The cow rolls its eyes, munching on grass,
Listening to fables while minutes just pass.

One day a fox dressed as a queen,
Tripped over a root, it was quite a scene.
With laughter erupting from every small critter,
The queen fox declared, "I'll still be a hitter!"

And so, in the ferns, stories take flight,
With laughter and folly from morn until night.
Fables they tell, both silly and grand,
In this leafy world, all laughter is planned.

The Enchanted Waiting Area

In a waiting room filled with odd, bright chairs,
A parrot spins tales of the wild and the bears.
A hedgehog is knitting, lost in a seam,
While a frog croaks gently, caught in a dream.

The clock on the wall makes a funny face,
As minutes meander, this isn't a race.
An octopus juggles, balloons up and down,
While the cat in the corner pretends to frown.

The chairs start to dance, with a cha-cha beat,
As laughter erupts, it's life's little treat.
A wizard appears, flipping cards in the air,
"Do you have a ticket? Well, do you dare?"

In this waiting area, fun is a path,
Bright colors, odd sounds, and delightful math.
With every strange moment, new stories are born,
In this whimsical place, no one feels worn.

Murmurs of the Leafy Stage

On the leafy stage, where the whispers flow,
A snail with a violin steals quite a show.
Beetles applaud, with their tiny little hands,
As crickets chirp beats to the magical bands.

A raccoon in a tux, slick as can be,
Tells jokes about food, like it's all for free.
The trees join the fun with rustling leaves,
And the sun shines brighter, just what it believes.

A dance-off erupts as the breeze starts to sway,
As flowers twist 'round in their colorful play.
Laughter surrounds like a glittering mist,
And every small creature is part of the gist.

So gather ye round to this leafy delight,
Where murmurs of fun dance into the night.
Enjoy the absurd, the whimsical rhyme,
On this leafy stage, let's savor the time.

Reverberations in the Glade

In the glade where whispers play,
Saplings giggle and sway.
Frogs in tuxedos, quite the sight,
Debate the moonlit night.

Crickets chirp in a raucous tone,
While squirrels dance on a shiny bone.
With laughter echoing through the trees,
A symphony of nature's tease.

Beneath a mushroom, a party spry,
The ants all dress in a dapper tie.
Their punch? A brew of honey and dew,
Who knew it would raise a hullabaloo?

So if you're lost and need a guide,
Join the revelry where critters hide.
Nature's jesters in full delight,
A glade of giggles, pure and bright.

The Untamed Script

In an attic filled with dusty dreams,
The raccoons plot their wild schemes.
A script of snacks and stolen gold,
Unfolding tales hilariously bold.

Tufts of fur in a role reversal,
The hedgehogs host an impromptu rehearsal.
Lines scratched out on leftover leaves,
They pause for laughter, as bellyache weaves.

The owl directs with a raspy hoot,
While rabbits hop in their best cute suit.
"Break a leg!" one fox deftly said,
And all took turns pretending they're dead.

Curtains of ivy drawn back with flair,
A cast of critters beyond compare.
Each act brings giggles to the rim,
In this wild world, we laugh on a whim.

Tales of the Leafy Veil

Underneath a leafy veil,
A gossip mill begins to sail.
Breezes carry secrets, oh so light,
As ladybugs take wing at night.

A squirrel prances with a nutty grin,
His friends all teasing, where have you been?
With every blush and banter bold,
Stories emerge just waiting to unfold.

A hedgehog tells a joke so sly,
It rolls off leaves and makes them cry.
While butterflies sip on wilted brew,
Cackling joy at a wild debut.

Under the stars, the tales are spun,
With wild laughter, the night's begun.
Each whisper, a giggle in the air,
In this leafy world, delight is rare.

Ballet of the Boughs

A dance where branches twist and twirl,
With acorns whirling in a carefree swirl.
Birds in tutus, perfect pirouette,
Nature's ballet, a comedic duet.

The wind plays music, a jaunty tune,
While flowers sway like they're in a cartoon.
With bees as soloists buzzing along,
They'll sing you a memorable song.

The groundlings chuckle at the leafy show,
As grasshoppers leap and put on a glow.
In this light-hearted dance of delight,
Every move is met with squeals of fright.

So come one, come all, join the fun,
In the dance of nature, under the sun.
With whimsy and laughter, the stage is set,
In the ballet of boughs, no regrets.

The Secret Garden's Oath

In the garden, gnomes do dance,
With floppy hats and no sense of chance.
Bees sip nectar, sipping with glee,
Watching squirrels plotting a spree.

Rabbits in coats are hosting tea,
While flowers gossip, oh so carefree.
A worm in a tux, he spins a fine tale,
While daisies whisper, with the wind's wail.

Petunias prance in the morning sun,
Declaring their bloom is second to none.
Yet tulips grumble, feeling quite blue,
At the jester bugs, they've always known too.

So here's the oath, in laughter we trust,
With blooms as witnesses, it's a must!
In this secret space, all's lighthearted fun,
Where every leaf dances 'til day is done.

Whispered Legends of Mossy Trails

On mossy trails, where shadows play,
The forest chuckles in a leafy way.
Old trees tell jokes, their bark's quite thick,
While mushrooms laugh at the sprightly trick.

A fox in glasses, reading a tome,
Claims wisdom's found beneath every dome.
The streams giggle, bubbling with cheer,
As frogs croak punchlines loud and clear.

A snail in a hat joins the debate,
Saying slow is the key to feel great.
While crickets improvise nightly tunes,
Under the watch of a big, bright moon.

So wander these trails, let joy prevail,
With every footstep, a laughter unveil.
In the whispers of leaves, old legends reside,
Of jests, jigs, and a marvelous ride.

Lullabies of the Leafy Refuge

In a leafy refuge, where critters reside,
The wind sings softly, like a dear guide.
A hedgehog hums, tucks in tight,
While fireflies twinkle, greeting the night.

Bamboo flutes play a gentle tune,
As wise old owls cast glances at the moon.
Squirrels rap in rhythm on tree bark,
Blending their beats with a dog's barking lark.

Crickets croon in a symphonic choir,
While branches sway, fueled by desire.
A raccoon crafts riddles, sharing the laughs,
In this cozy nook where mischief never halves.

So if you wander where laughter is rife,
Join in the lullabies, embrace the life.
In this leafy refuge, dreams come alive,
Where stories and giggles forever thrive.

The Pulse of the Overgrown

In the overgrown patch, chaos reigns supreme,
A salad of colors, a gardener's dream.
Vines twist and tangle, a knotty affair,
While daisies debate if they'll cut their hair.

Weeds throw shade at the flowers so prim,
Saying, "Lighten up, don't be so grim!"
Butterflies flutter in a comedic dance,
While blades of grass form a band, take a chance.

A chubby hedgehog attempts to run,
Wobbling awkwardly, he's just having fun.
While a dandelion puffs, claiming it's bold,
Shooting seeds like confetti, a sight to behold.

So here beats the pulse of nature's parade,
In the overgrown realm where pranks are made.
With each little creature playing its part,
A symphony of laughter, straight from the heart.

Whispers in the Loam

In a patch of soil, secrets sprout,
Worms gossip loudly, there's no doubt.
Cabbages chuckle, the radishes sing,
Nature's own stage, what joy they bring.

Rabbits dance, under moonlit streams,
Squirrels tell tales of their wacky dreams.
With acorn hats, they prance around,
A comedy show, lost and found.

Dirt-covered boots stomp in delight,
As beetles debate who's the best in flight.
Ladybugs laugh at the ants in line,
Each little critter, feeling divine.

Frogs croak sonnets, a musical flair,
While butterflies flutter, light as air.
In this loamy realm, the humor thrives,
Where even the soil giggles and jives.

Starlit Script

Under a blanket of twinkling stars,
The fox tells tales of his travels afar.
With a wry smile, he spins the yarn,
Of mischief and tricks, both cheeky and charmed.

The owls debate which way to fly,
While crickets weave laughter into the sky.
Beneath the moonlight, the stories unfold,
A thespian night, with antics bold.

Glowworms flicker like stage lights bright,
As raccoons perform in the soft twilight.
Each creature a star in this nighttime show,
With laughter and antics that steal the glow.

In this dark, playful theater of dreams,
Where even the shadows are bursting at seams,
Nature's a writer, with pages galore,
Each script more silly than the time before.

Shadows on the Forest Floor

With sunbeams dancing, a playful tease,
Shadows frolic under tall, green trees.
A fox trips lightly on leaves of gold,
While laughter echoes from tales untold.

Rabbits run circles, their feet in a blur,
As squirrels debate who's the biggest purr.
Mushrooms giggle in their speckled caps,
Joining in on the forest's mishaps.

The stumps tell stories of years gone by,
While ants march diligently, oh so spry.
With such a crowd, it's hard to ignore,
The humor that flourishes upon the floor.

Amongst the ferns, the wind starts to play,
Whispering jokes of an old, wise gray.
In this shadowed realm, laughter takes flight,
A comedic haven, both silly and bright.

Unwritten Lines in the Underbrush

With scribbles of green, the brush holds tales,
Of fairies and gnomes with mischievous trails.
Each twig a quill, writing stories unseen,
The paper is moss, where dreams have been.

A raccoon plots with a sly little grin,
To swipe some berries while others join in.
The log is a stage for those who can sing,
Join in the fun, let your laughter ring!

In this hidden nook, the world feels alive,
With snickers and giggles, we dwell and thrive.
The secrets we keep, in whispers they flow,
Crafting the mischief, that none can outgrow.

Let's dance through the bugs, and tease the breeze,
In this wild place, we do as we please.
For the lines that are unwritten, we happily tread,
In the underbrush laughter, our hearts will be led.

The Unseen Performance

Behind the curtains, we all scheme,
Tripping on dreams like a bad ice cream.
A dancer slips, a laugh erupts,
While the spotlight beams, mischief disrupts.

A juggling cat steals the show,
While backstage whispers create quite the glow.
The props revolt, they dance on their own,
And leave the actors feeling overthrown.

The script was lost, tossed like confetti,
Characters blend like flavors all petty.
A cactus wearing a tutu sways,
While everyone laughs at the odd ballet.

As curtains close, the cheers arise,
Who knew mishaps could be such a surprise?
In this unseen chaos of giggles and cheer,
Every performance brings a reason to beer!

Whispers of the Wisteria

Giggling flora in the moonlight glow,
Dance with the breeze, putting on a show.
Petals chatter, secrets they share,
Do prancing daisies have secrets to bare?

Wisteria sighs, 'we've seen it all,'
From first dates to epic stage fall.
As crickets play tunes like jazzy scribes,
The blooms gossip about all the vibes.

An actor once tripped, dressed as a tree,
Spoke to the flowers—quite absurd, you see!
While daffodils shake in uncontrollable fits,
Clutching their stems, they giggle in bits.

With each tickling wind, they spread their tales,
Of plays gone wrong and misfit males.
In wisteria's laughter, every voice cries,
'Life is a stage,' as they brightly reprise.

Mysteries of the Hidden Stage

Under the floorboards, a raccoon rehearses,
Ad-libbing lines while chewing through verses.
A broom's in the spotlight, taking its bow,
While all of the props stand and wonder how.

The walls have ears, or so they say,
Collecting the tales in the strangest way.
A shoe with a story, a hat full of dreams,
Echoes of laughter in bright moonbeams.

A curtain's whisper and secrets collide,
Of clumsy missteps, where talent can hide.
A misplaced mic brings a ruckus, a roar,
As the audience howls—'We want even more!'

In shadows they giggle, the ghosts of the past,
Sharing their dreams, making fun unsurpassed.
Each step and mishap creates such delight,
In the hidden stage, laughter feels just right.

The Sway of Silent Pines

In the calm of night, the pines disobey,
Swaying to tunes in a breezy ballet.
They whisper tales of actors daft,
And prankish squirrels with their usual craft.

"Watch out for the moon! It's quite the tease,"
Chortle the branches, "it dangles with ease."
A slapstick chase in a midnight jest,
As shadows jive on a fun-loving quest.

The thief of the stage is a wise old owl,
With laughter that echoes through nature's prowl.
In pines' merry sway, such a circus of fun,
Where every mishap brings giggles by the ton!

So dance with the pines, let your spirits take flight,
In this quirky forest, everything feels right.
For nature's performance is never mundane,
In swaying silence, hilarity reigns!

Beneath the Willow's Gaze

A squirrel stole my sandwich, quite bold,
He danced on a branch, a sight to behold.
With a wink and a nod, he took off in flight,
Leaving me wondering, what a silly plight.

The willow just chuckled, her branches all sway,
Her leaves whisper jokes; it's a funny old day.
I laughed at my loss, it's just food, after all,
Squirrels can't share, they tend to enthrall.

A picnic disrupted by nature's own flair,
The buzz of the bees gave my thoughts quite a scare.
Yet under that willow, with laughter and glee,
I found peace in chaos, so wild and so free.

So here's to the creatures that brighten our skies,
With antics and mischief, and shiny brown eyes.
Beneath the old willow, I learned how to smile,
In nature's grand circus, I stayed for a while.

Curtain of Ivy

A curtain of ivy that twists on the wall,
Hides secrets and stories that tickle and brawl.
The vines play peekaboo, gently they sway,
As I trip on the rug, in a most graceful way!

The ivy just chuckles, it knows all my slips,
Hiding my blunders, with leafy tight grips.
"Do you think they all saw?" I whisper in fright,
But the ivy just giggles, 'It's quite a delight!'

In the quiet of twilight, shadows will dance,
As critters and giggles join in for a prance.
With a flick of the leaves, let comedy soar,
Behind that green curtain, there's always much more.

So I'll bow to the ivy, my comedic muse,
With every good blunder, I gladly refuse.
The more that I trip, the more that I grin,
Life's best when we laugh, let the fun times begin!

Resonance of the Hidden Heart

In a dusty old attic, with dust bunnies round,
Lies the heart of a jester, long lost but found.
A grin full of mischief, a smile that's wide,
Echoes of laughter, in shadows they hide.

In the corners it whispers, with echoes of cheer,
Tickling my senses, the warmth draws me near.
With chuckles like wind chimes, sweet melodies play,
In the attic of memories, where laughter can stay.

The hidden heart knows all the funniest tales,
Of climbers and fallers, and accidental fails.
It resonates deeply, each story a spark,
Lighting up days that once felt rather dark.

So here's to the laughter that hides in our core,
To the echoes that linger, forever encore.
For with every heartbeat, we dance and we jest,
In the sweetness of humor, we're truly blessed.

Lullabies for the Lost Soul

Lullabies sung by a cat with a hat,
She croons to the moon, and purrs just like that.
Lost souls wander 'round, seeking warmth, seeking cheer,
As the cat whispers softly, 'You're safe, have no fear.'

In shadows they gather, like lost little sheep,
While the cat twirls and giggles, not ready for sleep.
With a flick of her tail, and a wink of her eye,
She serenades softly, under the night sky.

A chorus of chuckles from creatures unheard,
Spins tales of hijinks, with every soft word.
For in every lost heart, there's a light to be found,
With laughter and lullabies, love will surround.

So cuddle up close, let the laughter unfold,
For even lost souls enjoy stories retold.
In a world full of whims, where the funny games play,
We all have our melody, come join in the fray!

Reflections in a Mossy Mirror

In the pond, a frog takes a dive,
His reflection looks half alive.
With a croak that shakes the trees,
He splashes water, quite the tease.

A squirrel watches from its perch,
With a nut, it's ready to lurch.
Off the branch, it takes a leap,
While the frog goes back to sleep!

A rabbit hops by, asking why,
The frog just grins and waves goodbye.
"Life's a splash, come join the spree!"
Echoes of laughter, wild and free.

In the mirror, a friendship blooms,
Between the trees and playful tunes.
Nature's cheer, a jovial sight,
In this clearing, all feels right.

Echoes of a Hidden Sanctuary

In a grove, where jokes abound,
A wise old owl spins tales profound.
A rabbit rolls his eyes and snorts,
"Your puns are odd, but I love sports!"

A turtle nods, but takes his time,
"Why rush? I'm savoring this rhyme."
In the corner, a chatter unfolds,
A chipmunk boasts of treasures untold.

The echoes bounce, a playful race,
Where laughter dances, leaves embrace.
Secrets shared beneath the sun,
In a sanctuary of pure fun.

With every quip, the joy extends,
In this realm, all are friends.
The hidden echoes, sweet and bright,
Mark our moments in delight.

Beneath the Canopy's Heart

Beneath the leaves, a party grows,
A mouse in shades, striking a pose.
"Come dance with me, let's spin around!"
The forest floor, a lively ground!

A deer does joins, with nimble feet,
While a hedgehog hums a funky beat.
Together they twirl, what a sight,
Under the moon and soft starlight.

A raccoon sings in a raspy tone,
"Let's revel till we're overthrown!"
With every laugh, the shadows sway,
Beneath the heart, we dance and play.

In the twinkle of a firefly,
Every heart knows how to fly.
Beneath the canopy, joy imparts,
A woodland waltz, delighting hearts.

Soliloquies of a Forest Dream

In silence, the trees begin to chat,
"Did you see that? A chubby acrobat!"
A plump little owl takes a grand flight,
"Too much snack in the pale moonlight!"

The branches giggle, a rustling sound,
As twirling leaves spin round and round.
"Join the fun!" the whispers call,
Where dreams depart, but laughter's tall.

A sleepy bear snores with flair,
While critters gather, unaware.
"Imagine the pranks we could devise!"
Forest tales sparkle in our eyes.

Underneath the stars we scheme,
Crafting mischief in a dream.
In the soft hush of moonlit gleam,
The forest unfolds its funny dream.

Lanterns of the Garden's Shade

In the garden, a gnome takes a nap,
His hat's too big, it covers his cap.
The flowers giggle, they can't help but tease,
As bees do ballet on soft summer breeze.

A squirrel debates if the nut is too bold,
While ants march in line, their routine never old.
Nearby a frog croaks a nonsensical tune,
Underneath the glow of a luminescent moon.

A dance party erupts with a hint of surprise,
As fireflies twinkle like stars in the skies.
The lilies sway, their petals a whirl,
While a whimsical snail draws a spiral unfurl.

And when the sun rises, the laughter will fade,
The garden returns, a quaint masquerade.
For in this wild space, all worries are gone,
With lanterns aglow, till the break of dawn.

The Color of Silence

In a field of whispers, the daisies stand tall,
A crow tells a joke, but it trips on a stalk.
With petals blushing, the tulips take flight,
As laughter erupts from the carefree twilight.

A tortoise in spectacles reads from a book,
While crickets hold meetings beside babbling brook.
The quiet holds colors, a mischievous hue,
Where everything giggles, if only you knew.

While moths tell their secrets in flickering lights,
And shadows play tag until deep in the nights.
A raccoon with mischief gives all a delight,
As silence can shimmer, oh what a sight!

So come hear the silence, so vibrant and bold,
In a world full of laughter, where stories unfold.
With every moment wrapped in pure glee,
In this colorful hush, forever we'll be.

Enigmas in the Lush Retreat

Among tangled vines, a riddle's at play,
Where rabbits wear glasses and think they can sway.
A fox plays the harp for a crowd of lost frogs,
While toads croak the chorus under breezy logs.

The mushrooms hold secrets, all creaky and old,
As whispers and giggles from fairies unfold.
An owl in a cloak spins tales of the night,
And catches the dreams that escape in their flight.

With twilight as canvas, the stars start to wink,
A jester appears, with a jolly old drink.
He juggles the fireflies, flickering bright,
Till sleep sneaks in softly, bidding goodnight.

In the heart of the woods, where confusion is free,
The enigmas of nature play tricks on the glee.
So wander the lush, let laughter abound,
In a world of puzzles, where joy can be found.

A Sylvan Symphony

In the heart of the woods, a symphony starts,
With owls on violins, and squirrels with their charts.
The brass section blossoms from blowbugs nearby,
While the willow trees sway with a graceful sigh.

A raccoon rings bells made of twinkling dew,
And the crickets keep time with their rhythmical cue.
The frogs add a bass as they croak and they leap,
Creating a melody that lulls all to sleep.

The sunbeams are trumpets that shine through the leaves,
As nature's orchestra bows, and folks can't believe.
Everyone claps for the show of the year,
In the sylvan recess, where laughter is clear.

So gather your friends, take a seat on the grass,
For this funny affair shall never pass.
Let the melodies whirl as the laughter takes flight,
In the symphony's glow, all is perfectly right.

The Serpent's Whispering Leaf

In the garden where shadows play,
A serpent joked, "Let's dance today!"
His tail swirled with a surprising grace,
As flowers giggled and joined the chase.

The squirrels chuckled, tails in a knot,
"Is that a wig or a boastful plot?"
The serpent winked, with charm so sly,
"I'm just here for the laughs, oh my!"

A squirrel slipped, it was quite a sight,
As serpent roared, "You're not too bright!"
Then all fell silent, the trees did sway,
In laughter's grip, they danced away.

So if you wander in woods so dense,
Listen close, there's humor immense.
For nature's jesters, both sly and sweet,
Leave smiles behind where the shadows meet.

Illusions in the Leafy Domain

A leaf wore glasses, quite absurd,
It thought it wise, not just a bird.
"Come hither, friends, I'll show you tricks,
You'll laugh so hard, it'll make you sick!"

The ant marched up, shaking its head,
"Your style's confusing, I'll stick to my bread."
But the leaf then swirled, did a silly dance,
"Don't be shy, give laughter a chance!"

A caterpillar piped in with glee,
"Watch me wiggle, one-two-three!"
The forest echoed with joyous sounds,
With every giggle, the spirits found!

When shadows stretched and time was late,
The leaf declared, "Now that's first-rate!"
In leafy laughter, the night turned bright,
And dreams took off on wings of light.

Tales of the Forest's Embrace

Beneath the boughs where laughter thrived,
A band of critters had all arrived.
With acorns stacked and stories spun,
The night was young, let the games begun!

A raccoon declared, "I'm king of the show!"
With a crown made of leaves that put on a glow.
The others roared, "That's quite the hat!"
"Join me or leave," he said with a pat.

A wise old owl perched high above,
Said, "Laughter and friendship, that's what we love!"
With antics shared, the forest swayed,
In giggles and grins, the worries replayed.

So gather your pals, forget all the stress,
In the heart of the woods, we're all a success.
With tales of delight in the moon's soft grace,
Life's silly moments are hard to replace.

Fables from the Glistening Thicket

Once in a thicket, behind a stout tree,
Lived a fox who claimed, "I'm royalty!"
With a tuft of grass atop his red head,
He'd prance and pose, while others just fled.

A rabbit remarked, "Oh, what a sight!
A king of the woods, in the dead of night!"
But the fox just laughed, with a flick of his tail,
"I'm the life of the party, I'll always prevail!"

Then came a frog, with a ribbit so loud,
"Is that really a crown? You're not in a crowd!"
The critters joined in with roars and croaks,
In this playful jest, only laughter awoke.

So if you find yourself lost, quite roguish,
In the thicket alive with spirit and flourish,
Remember the fox and his whimsical guise,
In the fables of fun, let your laughter rise!

Secrets Beneath the Canopy

In leaves above, the squirrels conspire,
Whispering secrets of cheese-filled desire.
The raccoons laugh at a banana peel,
As shadows dance, they spin a surreal deal.

In this realm, laughter bursts like a balloon,
Where frogs debate under a merry moon.
A hedgehog tap dances, quite out of tune,
While crickets provide the wacky cartoon.

Mice play poker with acorn caps in tow,
Each wager raises, a carrot for show.
The owls hoot jokes that make no sense,
While beetles roll dice, it's all quite dense.

Silly stories unfold in the night,
As fireflies twinkle, and spirits take flight.
In this canopy of giggles abound,
The forest takes a bow, laughter resounds.

Enchanted Reflections

A pond glimmers like a disco ball,
Where frogs in tuxedos have the grandest ball.
Ducks glide by with a glamorous flair,
While fish giggle beneath, unaware of the pair.

Mirror, mirror, what's the latest trend?
The frogs croak loudly, "Fashion's to blend!"
A turtle in shades claims style's his game,
While a catfish struts in a delicate frame.

Swans gossip quietly, gliding with grace,
Pretending to know the latest in lace.
While mermaids above snicker and sing,
"Is that a feather? Oh, what a silly thing!"

In reflections, humor casts shadows so bright,
As twilight slips in, bringing giggles to light.
This enchanted world, a canvas of cheer,
Where laughter bounces, and joys reappear.

Hues of Abandon

In a vibrant patch where the wildflowers dance,
Lies a gnome stuck in quite a funny romance.
With butterflies flirting, he turns deep shade,
As rainbow colors splash, like winks they parade.

Grassy hills roll, tickled by breezy laughs,
Where unicorns munch on their pastel staffs.
And pixies giggle, casting funny spells,
As daisies debate on how sweetness dwells.

The sun throws confetti, bright rays in a fling,
While a grumpy old troll finds joy in the swing.
Clouds wear mustaches and heckle the day,
As giggles explode in a whimsical way.

In this realm, hues of mischief delight,
Where every corner twinkles with light.
Embrace every shade, let joy's anthem rise,
For laughter's the color that never denies.

An Ode to Velvet Dreams

In slumber's embrace, mischief takes flight,
As kittens waltz softly in dreams of delight.
Unicorns munch jellybeans in a spree,
While teddy bears giggle, lost in the sea.

A secret parade on a soft cloud swell,
Where snoring dragons ring the laughter bell.
Pillows wear smiles, plush laughter galore,
As quilted blankets whisper tales of yore.

In velvet dreams where silliness sings,
The moon throws a party with magical rings.
Sprinkling stardust on wayward thoughts,
As giggles in chorus, dance in the knots.

So take off your shoes, embrace every beam,
In this quirky land, forget what may seem.
With laughter as fabric, let's sew up the seams,
In an ode to the wonders of velvet dreams.

Conversations with Thorns and Leaves

In the garden where gossip grows,
Thorns complain of garden woes.
Leaves giggle in a breezy dance,
Whispering secrets, taking a chance.

The rose said, "You've pricked me so!"
The bush replied, "You steal the show!"
With every jab and teasing poke,
Laughter blooms, and thorns provoke.

Roots dig deep in earth's old lore,
Unruly vines yet crave for more.
"Let's start a club!" a leaf did shout,
But thorns just laughed and turned about.

A prickly union, what a sight!
With humor forged, they'll spark delight.
In this patch where laughter thrives,
Thorns and leaves grow joyful lives.

The Hidden Storyteller's Arc

Behind the bush, a tale unfolds,
A snail much wiser than it holds.
He spins a yarn with every inch,
While in the crowd, a squirrel's a cinch.

Tales of acorns lost, at a cost,
He claims he's the number one host.
Squirrels roll eyes, "What do you know?"
They hoard and scurry, putting on a show.

A rabbit hopped in, ears held high,
"Can one group tell tales? Oh my!"
The story got tangled, as voices raised,
They laughed till the sun faded, amazed.

A chorus of giggles, a poet's delight,
Where snails write slow and squirrels take flight.
Under the canopy, tales of the brave,
In laughter and friendship, they all misbehave.

Moonlit Musings in the Thicket

Under the glow of the silver moon,
Crickets chirp out a merry tune.
Owls blink twice; they join the fun,
In this thicket, all worries shun.

Rabbits gather with a snug embrace,
Jokes exchanging at a rapid pace.
A hedgehog grumbled, "Why such a fuss?"
"We're here to party! Join us or miss!"

The stars joined in with a twinkling grin,
As the night found its rhythm and spin.
The trees swayed gently, a playful dance,
Nature herself had entered the chance.

So in the thicket, the night won't cease,
With laughter and joy, they find their peace.
As dawn approaches, the tales leave traces,
Of moonlit nights and happy faces.

A Tapestry of Ferns and Dreams

In a tapestry woven of dreams and green,
Ferns whisper stories that few have seen.
With fronds held high, they plot and scheme,
Daring each other to chase a dream.

One fern proclaimed with zest and flair,
"I'll grow tallest, if you all dare!"
The mosses giggled, "Oh, what a sight!"
"Can you outgrow the moon tonight?"

A dandelion floated, shaking with glee,
"I'll send my wishes over to thee!"
Spinning stories of love and cheer,
Mirth in the garden, the ferns draw near.

So twirls a gust, as laughter sings,
In a dance of green where freedom springs.
A patch quite hearty, where dreams entwine,
In nature's humor, all friends align.

www.ingramcontent.com/pod-product-compliance
Lightning Source LLC
Chambersburg PA
CBHW070312120526
44590CB00017B/2649